W.i.t.c.h.

Will Irma Taranee Cornelia Hay Lin

FRIENDS

W.i.t.c.h

Will   Irma   Taranee   Cornelia   Hay Lin

FRIENDS

HarperCollins *Children's Books*

First published in the USA by Volo/Hyperion Books for Children.

First published in Great Britain in 2006 by HarperCollins Children's Books.
HarperCollins Children's Books is a division of HarperCollins Publishers Ltd.

The HarperCollins Children's Books website is at
www.harpercollinschildrensbooks.co.uk

© 2006 Disney Enterprises, Inc.

ISBN: 0-00-723267-5
ISBN-13: 978-000-723267-3

1 2 3 4 5 6 7 8 9 10

The HarperCollins Children's Books website is at
www.harpercollinschildrensbooks.co.uk

Printed and bound in Italy

Visit www.clubwitch.co.uk

CONTENTS

CHAPTER ONE
HOW TO SPOT A TRUE FRIEND

⑥ Saturday
Heatherfield Park

Irma: Isn't this great?

Will: What?

Irma: Lying in the middle of the park, just doing . . . absolutely nothing!

Hay Lin: Hmmm, you're right. . . .

Irma: Too bad hanging out isn't a subject in school.

Cornelia: You'd be at the head of the class, that's for sure!

Taranee: Um . . . I don't want to interrupt you, but I thought you came here to help me! You know that if I don't find that . . . monster, I won't be able to finish my science project.

Irma: Come on, Taranee! It's just a harmless little beetle, not some green, six-headed alien!

Will: Taranee's right. We did promise to help. Come on, let's get moving!

Taranee and Will get up, but the other three don't budge.

Irma: Yeah, yeah, sure . . . later.

Cornelia: Hold on a minute. . . .

Hay Lin: Can't we do it tomorrow?

Will: Some friends you are!

Cornelia: Can't we just take it easy for a second, Will? Plus, you shouldn't judge friends only on how willing they are to help you. There are lots of other things to consider.

Will: Like what?

Cornelia: A friend always tells you what she thinks.

Irma: Great. So if a complete stranger walks up to you on the street and calls you a hateful, spiteful, unbearable person, she's got to be your best friend!

Cornelia: Knock it off, Irma, you know what I meant.

Hay Lin: I understand what you are saying, Irma. It's not like you have to tell your friends everything. You could end up hurting her feelings. There's no law that says you have to tell a friend you don't like the way she dresses!

Cornelia: No, of course not. But if you see your friend at a party with a stain on her skirt, you'd tell her, right? Think of all the embarrassment you'd save her!

Will: I agree. A friend is always on your side, no matter what.

Hay Lin: A real friend is concerned about you – not what other people might think.

Irma: A true friend accepts you the way you are: she likes you because you're you. She doesn't waste her time trying to change you!

Taranee: A true friend cares about you, accepts you the way you are, never betrays you, tells you what she thinks, and, of course, is ready to lend a hand whenever you need help. Right?

Cornelia, Hay Lin, Will, Irma: Right!

Taranee: So, do you think one of you *friends* could put that theory into practise and help me look for that beetle . . . *now*???

THE ORACLE SAYS . . .

Sometimes the start of a friendship can be truly magical. Just remember – friendships almost always need time to grow into something really important: by sharing experiences, you'll get to know the other person better.

DEAR WILL

**Will sees all sides of a situation.
Check out her responses to
these letters.**

Dear Will,
My best friend has a cell phone.
Can I call her 24/7?
– Chatterbox

Dear Chatterbox,
A cell phone is great, but you should make sure that your friend likes to talk as much as you do. Some people don't like to chat on cell phones all day long.
Will

Dear Will,
How can you tell if someone is a loyal friend?
– Unsure BFF

Dear Unsure BFF,
Friends are not like dogs. You can't go to the park
and ask a friend to fetch a stick for you to see if
she's loyal. Finding loyal friends takes hard work!
🐸 Will

FRIENDSHIP IS . . .
JUST THE BEST!

CHAPTER TWO
WANTED: NEW FRIENDS

FROM HAY LIN'S DIARY:

◎ *Friday*

Oooh!!! I am so bored! I can't take it anymore!
Will and the others all left for the long holiday
weekend with their families, which leaves me
alone in Heatherfield. Time seems to be standing
still, and I don't know what to do. There's never
anything good on TV, and I'm even getting sick
of drawing. (Today I finished another sketch pad,
the third this month!)

◎ *Saturday*

My mother doesn't understand me. All she does
is bug me. She says to stop complaining and
make an effort to find new friends. As if it were
so simple! How am I supposed to do that: look
in the phone book and start calling people in

alphabetical order to ask them if they want to be my friend? No way!

⑥ *Sunday*

Today my mother forced me to go out. She gave me my Rollerblades and said not to come back inside for at least an hour – unless there was some kind of emergency, of course. Well, there was an emergency! I was skating along the boardwalk, and I guess I must have been a little distracted, because without realising it I went crashing right into a girl on a bike! We both fell down. Luckily I wasn't hurt, and neither was she, I think – but I must have looked like such a jerk! Some expert skater . . . I got up, mumbled, "sorry," and went right back home carrying my skates.

⑥ *Monday*

Guess what? I have a new friend! Her name is Sarah, and tonight she's coming with her parents to eat with us at the restaurant! Here's what happened: this morning I wanted to stay in my room and pout. I don't know how my mum did it, but she got me to spill the beans (when she wants, she can really be magical, too!). I told her all about what had happened yesterday. She consoled me, but then said I had been wrong to run off and that I should have stopped to talk to the girl. Then she gave me a mysterious look and added that nothing happens by chance. I went out to skate again, and five minutes later I met up with the same girl, right where we had crashed yesterday!

She came up to me and asked how I was. Without even realising it, we began talking. It turns out that Sarah is my age! She's here on holiday with her parents and was actually dying to make new friends, too!

THE ORACLE SAYS . . .

To make new friends, many times all you have to do is step outside your door and meet people. The important thing is not to be afraid to get out there and show the world who you are. Most people need friends just as much as you do.

FIVE TIPS ON MAKING NEW FRIENDS

WILL: Join a sports team. Being part of a team is a great way to make new friends.

IRMA: Try out for the school play. If you like to sing and dance, you would be having fun *and* making friends!

TARANEE: Become a member of a club. Many schools have clubs for photography, writing, and other hobbies.

CORNELIA: Take a class, in dance, art, or karate – find something that you'd like to learn more about.

HAY LIN: Volunteer. Read the local paper to find organisations that have volunteer opportunities for kids. You can help out – and make a new friend in the process!

FRIENDLY TIPS: Five Ways to Hit It Off with a New Friend

WILL: I would tell her about my dormouse – and all about the pets at Mr. Olsen's pet store. If she likes animals as much as I do, we'll be friends for sure!

IRMA: I would tell one of my best jokes – if she laughs, she's in!

TARANEE: I would ask her if she likes photography and see if we had other hobbies in common.

CORNELIA: I would ask her where she bought such cool shoes, because she would undoubtedly love fashion as much as I do!

HAY LIN: I would ask her if she wanted to do an art project with me. Art is a great "getting to know you" activity!

CHAPTER THREE
TOP-TEN...
FRIENDS?

⊙ *Thursday*

Hay Lin's house

Irma: I can't believe it! I'm only ten minutes late and the cookies are already gone!

Taranee: Come on, Irma, take it easy. Things could be worse.

Cornelia: For Irma? I don't think so!

Will, Hay Lin, Irma (together): Cornelia!!!

Cornelia: I was only joking.

Irma: Hmmpf! Anyhow, you said something about problems, Taranee?

Taranee: Nothing serious, it's just something I wanted to talk to you all about.

Irma: Go on, tell us everything!

Taranee: Well, you remember me talking about Bea, right?

Hay Lin: Sure. She went to your old school, before you moved here.

Taranee: She was my neighbour and my best friend. We always did everything together.

Will: Do you miss her?

Taranee: Yes, I do. . . . but we've been writing to each other. Yesterday she sent me an e-mail that was kind of upsetting.

Hay Lin: Did something bad happen to her?

Taranee: No, but she asked me a question that threw me. . . . She asked me whether she was still my best friend.

Cornelia: What did you tell her?

Taranee: Nothing yet. I mean, she's still special to me, but now you all are part of my life, too! I can't really say who my best friend is.

Hay Lin: Maybe she still is your BFF, since you've known her longest.

Cornelia: I don't think the answer's as simple as that, Hay Lin.

Irma: Maybe you should ask yourself who's been there for you when things were toughest.

Will: This is not a competition!

Hay Lin: 'Cause if it was, we would win, hands down! Think of everything we've been through together!

Taranee: Yeah, but . . . that's not all there is to it, right?

Irma: No, of course not. We also happen to be much nicer than anyone else. Well, there are always exceptions. Right, Cornelia?

Will: Oh, Irma, knock off the teasing!

Cornelia: You know what I say? I think it's Bea's question that's all wrong. You can't rank your feelings for people. You can have feelings and friendship with different people, and each one is special to you for a different reason.

Will: Or maybe you can rank your friends, but what are you going to do with a top-ten-friends list when what you really want to do is hang out with them, all of them, no matter who they are or what ranking they have?

Irma: Yeah, and a friend may still be special to you, even if she is a grouch sometimes.

Cornelia: You wouldn't be thinking of anyone in particular, would you?

Irma: No-o-o-o!

Taranee: I guess you're right. I can't rank Bea like some top-ten song. And besides, no one can compare to you guys!

DEAR IRMA

Irma always has something funny to say. Check out her witty answers to these questions.

Dear Irma,
How many friends should a person have?
– Carefully Counting

Dear Carefully Counting,
It depends. Try having a sleepover party, and invite as many friends as you have pillows! Just kidding. . . . There is no limit on friends. Just try to be a *good* one.
♥   Irma

Dear Irma,
I have two best friends. How do I know which is
the better friend?
– Double Duty

Dear Double Duty,
You could give them a test, but what would you
ask? Don't judge friends. You should be thankful
that you have double the friendship and fun!
💜 Irma

WHAT CAN YOU DO IF . . .

All of your friends have a problem they need help with at the same time?

- If you can, invite them all to your house for a big powwow. There's strength in numbers!
- Make a list of all the problems. Sometimes seeing the problems in print makes them more manageable.

You have two extra tickets to a show and at least four friends that you want to invite?

- Invite the two who you think would be most interested.
- Talk about it openly with them, and decide together what to do.
- Purchase the extra tickets necessary and split the total cost equally among all of you.

Your friends all have differing opinions on your look?

• Listen to all of them, think about what each has to say, then follow only the advice you really feel is best.
• Remember, the first thing is to please yourself.

Your friends don't share your interests?

• Try to get them involved in the things you like. You may end up changing someone's mind.
• Don't worry; it's only right that everyone has her own interests.

FRIENDSHIP FILES

You know that you're friends because . . .

- She makes you laugh even while you're crying.
- She's lots of fun and you have a great time together.
- She's strong and brave; you wish you could be like her.
- The two of you hit it off right away.
- You can talk for hours on the phone together.
- She always speaks the truth.
- She knows you so well she can practically read your mind.
- She would never, ever betray you.
- You've grown up together and she's almost like a sister.
- Well, just because!

CHAPTER FOUR

BEST FRIENDS FOREVER

FROM TARANEE'S DIARY:

Thursday

I am so excited! Annie's here for a visit! We've
been writing e-mails and talking on the phone
for months. Even though it's not the same as
being in school together, I'm glad that we've
stayed friends ever since I moved here to
Heatherfield. But now she's finally here with me,
and she's staying until Sunday.

The first thing we did was sit in my room and
catch up. I wanted to hear all about my old
school! Then I filled her in on Heatherfield
gossip, and then we got out my old diaries.
It was great going through the pages
full of secret codes that only we
can understand!

⑥ *Friday*

Annie and I spent this afternoon trading clothes, one of our favourite hobbies. Annie opened her suitcase, I started rummaging through my closet, and in five minutes the room looked as if skirts, pants, and T-shirts had invaded it! We've always traded everything: books, magazines, videos, CDs, and, of course, clothes, since we wear the same size. It used to drive our mothers crazy when they found clothes they'd never seen before in the wash. Today we traded two sweaters, a sweatshirt, and a jacket. Our poor mums – are they in for a few surprises next wash day!

P.S. Tomorrow is the opening of my favourite photographer's exhibit, and she'll be there, too! I'd like to take along some shots of mine and hear what she thinks. I wonder if Annie feels like going there with me.

⑥ *Saturday*

Annie came to the exhibit with me and it was amazing! I had my best shots with me, but when I saw the photographer, I just wanted to run away! She was surrounded by a crowd of people. I didn't think that I'd be able to get through.

Luckily, Annie took me by the hand and started to push forward with me: once we got there, I had to show my pictures. And guess what? The photographer complimented me and gave me tons of useful advice. Thanks a million, Annie! Annie gave me the right push and then let me go ahead by myself. With her standing by me and giving me her support, I dared to do something I'd never have had the guts to do alone.

⑥ *Sunday*

Annie left today, but I'm not too sad about it: after all, our friendship will never end! Everything we've done together and shared is a one-of-a-kind thing, and always will be. Our friendship is like a treasure that we'll keep for the rest of our lives. To tell the truth, saying good-bye to her did leave me feeling somewhat sad for a moment, but then, luckily, Hay Lin, Irma, Will, and Cornelia came by. We talked and laughed a lot, and the day wound up being a lot of fun. I LOVE ALL MY FRIENDS!

A FRIEND IS THE BEST WHEN . . .

The five girls give their answers.

IRMA: She can make you laugh while you're watching the latest tearjerker movie. With her, even crying can be fun!

CORNELIA: You're having a bad day and she takes you shopping to cheer you up.

TARANEE: She helps you come up with the right plan to win a boy's heart. Even if it doesn't work, you'll have lots of laughs!

WILL: She invites you over to take a break from your math homework: after a walk together, even equations become bearable!

HAY LIN: She takes you out for an ice-cream cone after you've bombed out on your history test.

CHAPTER FIVE
THE REAL DEAL

⑤ *Tuesday*
Recess at Sheffield Institute

Irma: With this math quiz coming up, I've lost my appetite. Anybody want my snack?

Will: No, thanks.

Taranee: I'm fine.

Cornelia: Sorry, I'll pass on it, too. Surely, somebody else will take you up on it . . .

Hay Lin: Irma, do you want my snack instead? It's a chocolate-chip cookie, your favourite.

Irma: Hmmm. No, thanks. What's the matter? Why are you all looking at me like that?

Cornelia: It's not like you to turn down a cookie!

Will: Are you sure you're feeling all right?

Irma: Yes, yes . . . I was just thinking.

Taranee: What's wrong?

Irma: Nothing. Well, I just witnessed a really bad scene.

Will: What was it?

Irma: You know Paula, right?

Hay Lin: Yeah, the one who plays volleyball with us? She's cool.

Cornelia: Oh, yeah. She's best friends with Joanna and Wanda. They're in one of my classes, and Paula always helps them out with their homework.

Irma: Yeah. Very generous of her, right? Too bad those two don't deserve it!

Will: **What do you mean?**

Irma: Well, yesterday was Paula's birthday, and guess what her two best friends did?

Hay Lin: **I guess they gave her something special.**

Irma: Those two didn't even wish her a happy birthday! Paula was crushed.

Cornelia: **Wow.**

Taranee: Poor Paula! It seems like Joanna and Wanda take advantage of her friendship.

Hay Lin: **Maybe we should talk to Paula.**

Will: Actually, we don't know all the details. Maybe they had some argument, or maybe they just forgot it was her birthday.

Cornelia: **Maybe what we should do is ask Paula what she thinks of Joanna and Wanda.**

Irma: You know what I think is really bothering me? This whole thing made me feel guilty about Martin. I don't think I ever took advantage of him, but I've often asked for his help. Especially in French class.

Taranee: **Okay, but you must have returned the favour.**

Irma: I'm not so sure.

Hay Lin: But if he asked you for a favour, you would do it, right?

Irma: I guess so. But I don't know if I could help him out as much as he's helped me!

Cornelia: Maybe he just liked spending that time with you. I mean, isn't that what he wants more than anything else? I think you've already given him more than you ever owed him.

Will: Aren't you going a little overboard? You can't measure friendship on a scale. It's not like, "I did this for you, now you do the same for me, otherwise it means you're taking advantage." It sure would be sad if you had to keep track of every favour you did a friend!

Cornelia: No, but if it's always the same person who gives, and always the same one who takes, then there's something wrong.

Taranee: Yup. Friendship isn't a one-way street.

Will: You're right, friendship is definitely a *two*-way street. But you should do a favour for a friend if you want to, not because you're expecting something in return.

Irma: You're right. I hope Paula's situation works out. All that talking brought back my appetite. Hay Lin, I'll take that cookie after all.

WHAT CAN YOU DO IF . . .

You think one of your friends is taking advantage of you?

- Ask yourself what your friend's real intentions are. If you know they are good, then there's no problem!
- Remember, she could be going through a rough time, and she might need your attention.
- If you're still not sure where you stand, talk to her about how you are feeling.

Your friend asks you to do something that makes you uncomfortable?

- Refuse. Friendship is not a contract that obligates you to do anything you don't want to do!
- Discuss your thoughts openly with your friend. If she can't see your side of the story your friendship with her may need to be reevaluated. It's simple. Don't let anyone make you feel uncomfortable!

You think you're taking advantage of a friend?

• Take it easy. The fact that you're wondering about it means that, more than likely, you're not really doing anything wrong.
• Write your friend a letter to let her know how much you appreciate her. It's a way of saying thanks.

DEAR HAY LIN
Hay Lin can see the lighter side of things, but she still gives great advice!

Dear Hay Lin,
When does friendship end?
– Curious

Dear Curious,
Let's see: F-R-I-E-N-D-S-H-I-P. It's over when you get to the P. Just kidding! Friendship can last forever – if you take special care. . . .
 Hay Lin

Dear Hay Lin,
Can friends be recycled?
– Wondering

Dear Wondering,
Sure, as long as you learn to separate the trash! Sometimes people change. It's good to keep an open mind!
Hay Lin

Dear Hay Lin,
Why do my friends act differently in a group?
– Teammate

Dear Teammate,
It's a lucky thing they do. It would be pretty
boring if they were all the same! How could you
tell them apart?
 Hay Lin

Dear Hay Lin,
Is your newest friend better than your other friends?
– Newbie

Dear Newbie,
No, she's just new. Don't judge friendships by
length. What makes friendships good is the
quality of the time friends spend together.
Hay Lin

31

CHAPTER SIX
FRIENDSHIP NO-NO'S

FROM IRMA'S DIARY

☺ Sunday

I'm about to explode!!!!! I try to be nice, but I have my limits, too! And my cousin Julie has definitely pushed me beyond those limits. She got here today and is staying until Friday. I don't know how I'll be able to put up with her until then. When we were little we used to be the best of friends, but now I can't stand her! Today, for example, Taranee came by to say hi, and as soon as she left Julie began making snide remarks about her, like: "Your friend dresses like a boy. Of course, to wear certain clothes you need to have the right body . . . like mine." I was shocked. Who does she think she is, judging people like that??? I tried to explain this to her without arguing, but it was useless.

⑥ *Monday*

Here we go again. . . . Miss Stuck-up strikes again! Today we went to the coolest hair salon in Heatherfield. We spent the entire afternoon there. When the stylist finished with me and I looked in the mirror, I must say, I thought I looked great. Then Julie – who in the meantime had gotten this horrendous updo – looked at me with a glare and said: "The cut's not bad, but it would look better on someone with more delicate features." At first I was floored, but luckily everyone at home liked my new do and complimented me on it (even Christopher!). Julie, however, continues to make a face every time she looks at me. If she doesn't cut it out, tonight I'll dye her hair lizard green while she's sleeping!

⑥ *Wednesday*

I can't take it anymore! Julie's driving me nuts. If it were up to me, I'd pay her cabfare and send her home right now. She never shuts up. She judges others as if she were perfect – only she's not, not at all. She's unable to put herself in anyone else's shoes. She's totally insensitive and hasn't got a clue as to what it means to listen.

⑥ *Thursday*

Tonight something incredible happened! Julie knocked on my bedroom door. At first she just wanted to chat, but then she began apologizing for the way she had been acting. She basically admitted that I had been right to criticise her, because sometimes she tends to get a little mean. She said that she winds up feeling guilty and never knows how to fix things. Then all of a sudden she burst into tears! She has no other friends and doesn't want to lose me. Seeing her cry like that made me realise that despite everything, I do care about her. So I put my arms around her and told her about how I believe that you can't have friends if you're not willing to be a friend yourself! I hope she really got the message. Anyway, tomorrow she's going home. We'll see if she has caught on the next time she comes to visit. But if she acts the way she's acted on this trip, I'm going to seal her mouth shut with duct tape!

THE ORACLE SAYS . . .

Nobody's perfect. Remember that when a friend makes you mad, or when you make her mad!

FIVE WAYS TO HOLD ON TO FRIENDS

WILL: When I have a comment, I make sure that it's constructive.

IRMA: I cover my mouth before I say what I think!

TARANEE: I tell it like it is – but first I remind her I'm a friend.

CORNELIA: I know when a friend needs to talk . . . and when she wants to be left alone.

HAY LIN: I practise saying, "I'm sorry."

FRIENDLY TIPS:
Ten Ways to Lose a Friend

1. Disappear into thin air when you know she needs you.

2. Criticise everything she says and does.

3. Criticise her other friends.

4. Always point out how perfect you are.

5. Point out all the mistakes she makes.

6. Flirt with the boy she likes.

7. Don't return her phone calls.

8. Don't save her a seat at lunch.

9. Tease her, especially in public.

10. If she tells you a secret, get it published in your local newspaper.

CHAPTER SEVEN
MISSION: MAKING UP

⊙ *Sunday*
Heatherfield boardwalk

Hay Lin: **Will!**

Will: Hi, Hay Lin! Isn't this a beautiful day?

Hay Lin: **Yes! Good thing it's Sunday. It'd be torture to have to go to school on a day like today!**

Will: You said it! The others aren't here yet. How about an ice cream while we wait?

Hay Lin: **Do you even have to ask? Sounds good to me! It's a lot easier to talk with an ice-cream cone in your hand.**

Hay Lin: Can I ask you for some advice?

Will: **Sure! About what?**

Hay Lin: It's about Vivian, a friend of mine from when I was really little. Sometimes we still hang out together. In fact, yesterday she came over to my house to ask me a favour.

Will: **What was that?**

Hay Lin: Since she knows that I

draw, she gave me a photograph of her and Denise, her best friend, and asked me to do a drawing of them.

Will: **Wow! She commissioned you to do a portrait, like a real artist! That's amazing.**

Hay Lin: It is, but the problem is that she needs my drawing to get her out of a tight spot.

Will: **What?**

Hay Lin: A few days ago she had a fight with Denise, and she hasn't spoken to her since. Vivian was the one who started it, and when she realised her mistake, she wanted to make it up to Denise, only she didn't know how. I didn't know what to tell her. What do you think?

Will: **Hmmm . . . Giving Denise a portrait of the two of them seems like a good idea. That way, Denise'll know that she still means a lot to Vivian. Maybe Vivian could write her a letter, too, if Denise isn't speaking to her.**

Hay Lin: Do you think it would help?

Will: **Sure it would, especially if Vivian understands that she was wrong! If you make a mistake, you've got to be big enough to apologise.**

Irma arrives at the boardwalk.

Will: **Irma, good timing! We need another brain**

here to help us figure this out.

Irma: As long as you're not talking about homework, I may be able to help.

Hay Lin: This has nothing to do with school. How do you win back a friend you've just had a big fight with?

Irma: First tell me what I win, and I'll explain everything to you.

Hay Lin and Will (together): Irma!!!

Irma: Okay, okay . . . just joking! The same thing happened to me with my cousin not too long ago. There was one thing I learned. It takes a lot of courage to talk about a problem and to apologise, but it takes even more to really listen.

Hay Lin: You sound like Mrs. Rudolph when she's explaining a new theorem! What do you mean?

Irma: What I mean is that no one's ever completely right. There are always two sides to a story. If you try to talk about what's on your mind, then you have to accept what the other person says, even if you don't agree.

Will: You mean you may find out you were not right at all?

Irma: That's it. The point is that just by talking to a friend you may end up realising you're wrong: you may learn something about yourself you'd never find out otherwise.

Hay Lin: Mmmm. That makes it sound as if fighting were a good thing!

Irma: Well, if by fighting you mean talking, and especially listening to each other, then, yes. I'd say "fighting" like this should be mandatory, at least once a month!

Will: You've got to be . . .

Irma: Why not! We could even set up rules. We could ban the use of offensive weapons like thick French dictionaries, smelly old sneakers . . .

Will, Hay Lin (together): Irma!!!

Irma: Oh . . . just joking!

THE ORACLE SAYS . . .

It's impossible to get along perfectly every day, so try to keep an open dialogue going with your friends. That way, you can come up with solutions to problems before they get worse.

DEAR TARANEE

Taranee loves to read and to have a good time. Her responses to these letters are thoughtful and funny!

Dear Taranee,
I'd like to give my friend flowers. What do you think?
– Best Bud

Dear Best Bud,
All flowers are fine, except cactus! You don't want to be a prickly friend!
✳ Taranee

Dear Taranee,
Is it okay to write an e-mail instead of calling a friend?
– Wired

Dear Wired,
You are a very modem friend! As long as your friend likes getting e-mails as much as you like sending them, you two are webbed to be together!
✳ Taranee

Dear Taranee,
Why can't I say I'm sorry to a friend over the phone?
– Tongue-tied

Dear Tongue-tied,
Maybe you've got the wrong number! Seriously, you should try to see your friend in person. Your apology will mean more delivered face to face.
✳ Taranee

Dear Taranee,
My friends and I are like animals when we fight. Is that bad?
– Catfighter

Dear Catfighter,
Only if you bite and scratch! Maybe you should try talking to each other instead? You might start fighting less.
✳ Taranee

FRIENDLY TIPS:
Advice for Having a
Constructive Argument

- Don't get mad right away. Try to listen first.

- Don't criticise her as a person. It's better to say, "I think you told me a lie" than "You're a liar."

- Make sure each of you gets a chance to understand the other side of the story.

- Be sincere, and gather up the courage to speak your mind.

- No insults allowed: that's the quickest way to lose a friend.

- Don't take it for granted that you know how she will respond to what you are saying. She may surprise you.

- Listen hard to what she has to say, rather than thinking up a reply while she's talking.

CHAPTER EIGHT
WHEN JEALOUSY STRIKES

☽ *Monday*
On the way to school

Cornelia: **Will! Will! Hey, Will Vandom . . . WAKE UP!**

Will: Uh . . . hi, Cornelia. I didn't hear you!

Cornelia: **I could see that! It looks like you're still sleeping!**

Will: I stayed up late last night writing to Lisa. . . .

Cornelia: **Your friend from camp last summer?**

Will: Yes. We used to have some great talks at camp, and we still write to each other. The funny thing is, we never agree on anything, which is probably why we love talking to each other. It makes for an interesting conversation!

Cornelia: **I guess yesterday's letter really got you worked up. . . .**

Will: Yeah. Lisa asked me what I thought about being jealous.

44

Cornelia: What do you mean?

Will: You know, when your best friend finds another friend and it leaves you feeling hurt. It happened to her. She's over it now, but she said that at the time she felt as if she had been betrayed.

Cornelia: It happened with me and Elyon, when we started hanging out with Hay Lin and Irma. We both got jealous. It's not a good feeling.

Will: Having a new friend doesn't mean your old friend isn't special anymore.

Cornelia: Yeah, I guess so, at least in theory. It's true that over time you realise that it's not that your relationship with your best friend has changed, it's that your circle of friends has gotten bigger and now includes other people. And there's a good chance that those people might be pretty cool, too. But . . .

Will: But what?

Cornelia: But when it happens, it can be hard. At first you can't believe your best friend wants to share secrets with someone else that she once shared only with you.

Will: Come on . . . it's not the end of the world! I think you're exaggerating.

Cornelia: I wouldn't say that. Elyon and I fought

about this a lot. It was a good thing we both liked Hay Lin and Irma. Otherwise it would have been a total disaster!

Will: Gee, Cornelia, it's hard for me to imagine you being jealous!

Cornelia: Thanks for the compliment, but I was very jealous.

Will: Really? I don't understand how such a normally levelheaded, rational person like you could ever feel like that. You know that a friend isn't a piece of personal property, right?

Cornelia: Of course, I do. But I felt hurt just the same.

Will: How did you and Elyon finally work things out?

Cornelia: We talked about it for a long time. We promised each other that our friendships with others would never interfere with our own. We even made a plan.

Will: What's that?

Cornelia: We began inviting Irma and Hay Lin out with us once in a while. And we made sure certain things between us would never change: like a phone call before going to bed.

Will: That's nice.

Cornelia: It worked. No more jealousy!

WHAT CAN YOU DO IF . . .

Your old friend is jealous of your new friend?

WILL: Talk to your old friend and explain to her that she's just as special to you as she was before. Be strong and insist on the two friends getting to know each other. Maybe ask them to hang out together, with or without you!

Your friend doesn't like your new friend at all?

CORNELIA: Well, you can't force two people to like each other, so you could hang out with each friend separately. Be diplomatic, and try to include both friends in plans – it might be fun!

You feel like an intruder in an old two-way friendship?

TARANEE: If your new friend's friend gives you dirty looks, be patient, and give her the reassurance that she needs to know that you're not there to steal her best friend away.

DEAR CORNELIA
Cornelia gives solid advice!

Dear Cornelia,
A friend of my best friend's second-best friend asked
me to be her best friend. What do you think?
— Friendly

Dear Friendly,
Sounds like a real tongue twister! Saying you
have a best friend is great, but being one is a
different story. Remember that actions speak
louder than words.
❀ Cornelia

Dear Cornelia,
At the pool I met this great girl I really get along
with. I'd like to have her join my friends for a
sleepover. Do you think it's a good idea to mix
friends?
— Swimmer

Dear Swimmer,
Yes! I'm all for my friends getting to know one
another. It's fun to have a large group of
friends!
❀ Cornelia

Dear Cornelia,
If a friend is jealous of another friend, is she still
a real friend?
— Confused

Dear Confused,
Yes. And she has real feelings, too! You should talk to your friend and try to let her know you like having more than one friend.
🌸 Cornelia

Dear Cornelia,
I can't stand friends who always agree with me.
– Me, Too

Dear Me, Too,
I totally agree! Oops, sorry! Just make sure that your friends know that different opinions are okay. Maybe they're nervous that you'll get mad when you disagree.
🌸 Cornelia

TEST

Your best friend has a new friend. How do you react? Take this quiz and find out how true a friend you are.

1. You and your friend are talking when her new friend comes up to you. You . . .
   A. Give her an evil look and turn your back.
   B. Ignore her and don't say a word.
   C. Smile, and say hello.

2. How would you describe the new friend?
   A. An unbearable pain!
   B. Worse than an unbearable pain!
   C. She's kind of a pain, but not a complete monster.

3. You have two tickets to a concert and your friend is sick. You . . .
   A. Skip the concert and go visit your sick friend.
   B. Give the two tickets to the new friend, and then go visit your sick friend. That way you're sure you won't be interrupted.
   C. Go to the concert with the new friend.

You've got a feeling that the new girl isn't being onest with your friend. You . . .

   A. Tell your friend that her new friend is a liar.

   B. Set up a trap to catch the liar in the act.

   C. Think that you could be wrong. You don't say anything.

5. Why not try to get to know your friend's new friend?

   A. You've got to be kidding!

   B. Great idea: learning her weak points could come in handy!

   C. In time, you never know. . . .

6. Are you jealous of the new friend?

   A. Of course! She'd better not steal my best friend.

   B. How could I be jealous of someone like her?

   C. Well . . . a little.

7. The new friend's worst quality?

   A. She's always butting in between my friend and me.

   B. Oh, she's got plenty!

   C. Like everybody, she's got her faults. But at least she's got good taste in friends.

8. Your old friend and her new friend stop hanging out together, and you end up becoming friends with the new girl. You . . .

    A. Jump for joy – too bad for your old friend.

    B. Can't answer. You would never become friends with her!

    C. Wonder what's wrong with hanging out with the new girl once in a while?

ANSWERS

You answered mostly A.

Intolerant

No matter how hard you try, you can't deal with this interference between you and your friend. And you can't even fake it. You don't like the intruder. You're well aware that jealousy is making you very green, but you have no desire to change your attitude.

You answered mostly B.

All-out War

Your friend is YOURS, and you don't like sharing. No one is allowed even within shouting distance. The intruder is an annoyance, and ntil she's out of the picture it will be a big battle between you and them.

You answered mostly C.

A Ray of Hope

You accept the new friend even if you don't know what to make of this person barging into your life. You respect your friend's choices, and this is proof of your loyalty. You try to look at the newcomer as not so much a bothersome intruder but a person with good and bad points . . . like all of us!

Dead Heat

The jury's still out. You still haven't made up your mind whether the intruder is a good thing or a bad thing for you. You're watching her moves along with your friend's, just to see how the situation unfolds. You'll decide on a strategy after you've gotten the whole picture.

CHAPTER NINE
WHEN A FRIENDSHIP ENDS

FROM CORNELIA'S DIARY:

⊚ *Tuesday*

Lucy, one of my skating friends, asked me to come to her house tomorrow afternoon. Her invitation kind of shocked me, because since I've known her, we've talked three, maybe four times, no more. I thought she and Maria, her best friend, were joined at the hip. Could something be up with them? I can't wait till tomorrow to find out!

⊚ *Wednesday*

At last I know what's going on. I spent the afternoon at Lucy's and she told me what happened. What a sad story! She and Maria got into a big fight over Thomas, this guy Lucy really likes. Maria didn't invite Lucy to a party that

Thomas was going to. When Lucy found out, Maria told her that she hadn't said anything about it because Lucy was too immature. But they're the same age! Lucy's feelings are hurt. More than just feeling bummed about missing a party, her friend, whom she completely trusted, had really hurt her feelings.

⑤ *Thursday*

Last night I did a lot of thinking. Lucy's story made me think about what had happened between Elyon and me, and how bad I felt when it looked as if she had turned her back on me. Of course, things got cleared up, and we became closer than ever. But when I thought that she had betrayed me, it seemed as though the whole world were crumbling before my eyes!

⑤ *Friday*

I saw Lucy at skating . . . she was really down in the dumps. She and Maria tried to talk it over, but it was a total failure. Now Maria doesn't want to have anything more to do with Lucy, because she says Lucy still acts like a little girl. Maria says that she's grown up and is much more mature than before.

⑥ *Saturday*

Today I went to the park with Lucy, and, boy, did she explode. She thinks she'll never be able to trust a friend again. Then I told her about what had happened between Elyon and me (well, I had to leave out some magical details!). In the end, we both came to the conclusion that one friend's betrayal doesn't mean you have to lose faith in friendship in general, because true friendship becomes stronger despite changes. And if Maria is going to be so insensitive and selfish, well, Lucy's better off without her!

I invited Lucy to come over tomorrow for hot chocolate with the girls and me. This will give her a chance to see that the world is full of some very special people. The five of us are a perfect example!

Betrayal is one of the worst things in the
world, because it leaves you feeling that
you can't trust anyone. But that's just not true.
For proof of this, you'll need the courage to open
yourself up to new experiences and place your trust
in new friends.

FIVE TIPS FOR SURVIVING WHEN A FRIEND LETS YOU DOWN:

WILL: I treat myself to a mega-cuddle with my dormouse!

IRMA: I call up my other friends to have some fun together!

TARANEE: I fly into a rage, then vent my anger by shooting basketballs!

CORNELIA: She does not deserve my friendship!

HAY LIN: I draw funny pictures until I burst out laughing!

CHAPTER TEN

WHEN YOU'RE IN THE MIDDLE

FROM WILL'S DIARY:

⊙ *Monday*

Here we go again! Irma and Cornelia have had another fight! Here's what happened. . . .
Cornelia was having a bad day, the kind where it's better to keep your distance if you don't want her to bite you. We all understood that right away – well, all of us except Irma (nothing new!). She kept on teasing until Cornelia finally snapped and said that if she'd wanted to spend the afternoon listening to baby talk, she would have gone to hang out with her little sister, Lilian, and her nursery-school friends. Irma took offense. "If you think you're so grown up," she said, "you shouldn't be wasting time with us little kids." At that point Cornelia got up and

stormed away without even saying good-bye to the rest of us. Great way to start out the week . . .

⑥ *Tuesday*

HELP! Today at school I felt weird talking to Irma and Cornelia. I didn't want either one to get offended. I didn't want to take sides. I actually think that they are both wrong. Cornelia does have an attitude, but Irma doesn't always know when to stop fooling around. They kept looking at each other as if they were about to fight, which made me pretty nervous. What I need is a plan to get them to make up, but I haven't got a clue! I'm going to go for a swim and see if I can't come up with something.

⑥ *Wednesday*

Yesterday I told Joan, the swimming instructor, about what had happened between Irma and Cornelia. I didn't think she would understand, but she turned out to be a super-expert. She told me it happens all the time on sports teams. She gave me a good piece of advice: the best way to make people get along is to point out all the things they have in common, get them involved in something they both like, and then let them handle the rest, without getting in the way. But what do those two have in common, besides their friends, of course? That's it! I know! The solution is our very own magical friendship. In a few days it'll be Hay Lin's birthday. How about a surprise party? Neither Irma nor Cornelia will be able to refuse. Tomorrow I'll see what Taranee thinks of the idea.

⑥ *Thursday*
Taranee and I came up with a super plan during school today. We'll tell Irma and Cornelia separately about Hay Lin's party. Then, at the right moment, we'll just happen to disappear, leaving the two of them alone.

⑥ *Friday*
IT WORKED! Taranee told Irma that she couldn't go shopping, and I told Cornelia that I couldn't go, so Cornelia and Irma wound up at the supermarket buying stuff for the party themselves. They ended up walking out of the store arm in arm. (Taranee and I had to spy!) Now I'd say it's time for a great party to celebrate Hay Lin's birthday *and* the real friendship of all of us in W.I.T.C.H. We're more united than ever!

FRIENDLY TIPS:
Helpful Advice about Dealing with Two Friends in an Argument

WILL: I never take sides, but I do say what I think!

IRMA: I tell a few jokes to try to lighten the situation!

TARANEE: I invite them both over for a snack and a chat.

CORNELIA: I give my opinion: that both of them are making a big mistake!

HAY LIN: I act as messenger, delivering their notes, and I add comments of my own!

CHAPTER ELEVEN
ALL FOR ONE!

⑥ *Friday*
Heatherfield Park

Irma: **TGIF, girls!**

Hay Lin: Here comes the weekend. Yippee!

Will: **Let's do something. I'm up for a super Saturday!**

Cornelia: How about shopping?

Irma: **Sounds great! You guys can come with me to get the latest Karmilla CD!**

Taranee shakes her head with a sigh.

Taranee: Sorry, but I've got plans.

Irma: **Nothing too exciting, I guess, judging by the expression on your face!**

Taranee: Not really. I have to go to the Grumpers' to finish a history project.

Cornelia: **Poor Taranee! Spending an afternoon with the grumpiest sisters in the world!**

Taranee: Don't remind me. I had to

go yesterday, too. It's torture to hang out with them!

Hay Lin: **Why? What did they do?**

Irma: Their favourite sport is badmouthing everything and everybody!

Taranee: **Uncool. They are like snakes in the grass.**

Cornelia: And the victims of their poison?

Taranee shakes her head.

Cornelia: **Come on, out with it, Taranee. Don't worry, their poison doesn't affect us! Who were they dissing?**

Taranee: Um . . . all four of you.

Hay Lin: **WHAT?**

Irma: Let's hear it! If those snakes have it in for us, we have the right to know what they said.

Taranee: **Okay, okay. Irma, they say you're nothing but a clown; Cornelia thinks she's all that, just because she's pretty; Hay Lin looks like a nut with those goggles of hers; and Will is shy to the umpteenth power.**

Will: Well, it's not as bad as I thought!

Taranee: **I kind of agree. In fact, being so different helps us get along well.**

Irma: Right! Girls like the Grumper sisters can only dream of a friendship like ours.

Hay Lin: **I bet they say things like that just because they're green with envy: I'm sure** they can see that we have much more fun when we hang out than they do.

Cornelia: So they try to break us up behind our backs.

Taranee: **Let them try, they're just wasting their energy!**

Cornelia: By the way, since Taranee was so brave in defending us against the Grumpers, I think we owe her a favour.

Irma: **Like? Going to their house with her . . . armed with swords and daggers?**

Will: Of course not. All we have to do is go together to pick her up after they finish their work!

Taranee: **Now that's a great idea! A half hour together with you guys will change my whole mood!**

Irma: And if we go get a nice double-chocolate cone together, the anti-Grumper effect is guaranteed!

FRIENDLY TIPS:
Friends Forever!

- Your group of friends shouldn't ignore the rest of the world. Welcoming in new people means a chance to grow and to learn.

- As a good friend, you should defend your friends from gossip that isn't true.

- It's best not to have secrets within a group.

- Decisions should be made together, always respecting the opinions of each group member.

- If you argue with one of your friends, try to work things out without getting the others involved.

DEAR IRMA
Irma is the jokester
of the group. She tries
to make everyone laugh.

Dear Irma,
Should friends tell each other everything?
– Need to Know

Dear Need to Know,
Yes! Don't forget "Hi" and "Thanks" and "You're great!" as well as any other words you like in the dictionary.
♥ Irma

Dear Irma,
Do we have to clang swords when we shout, "All for one and one for all"?
– One of Three

Dear One of Three,
Yes, according to tradition. But you might want to do it with hairbrushes, not swords!
♥ Irma

Dear Irma,
My friends always talk behind my back. Why don't they have the courage to say what they want to my face?
– Feeling Blue

Dear Feeling Blue,
Don't turn your back! If you feel that way, ask your friends. Talking is usually the best way to solve a problem.
 Irma

CHAPTER TWELVE
SOS FRIENDSHIP

FROM HAY LIN'S DIARY:

Saturday

Help! It's an Irma emergency!!! Today she dragged me around half the city, from store to store, looking for a dress for her cousin's party next week. We couldn't find anything, mainly because she had no idea what she really wanted. She wasn't happy with anything she tried on – one skirt was too long, another too short. The she liked the colour of one, but not the material, etc. And she kept saying over and over again, "I'm a beast, nothing looks good on me." I told her it wasn't true, that she was being too hard on herself, but . . . I couldn't convince her. When we left the store, she was megadepressed.

⑤ Sunday

Irma's still all upset and into her I'm-ugly-and-no-good routine. I tried to cheer her up, joking that she did have a problem – her eyesight! If she thinks she's ugly, it's only because her eyes don't work right. What other explanation could there be? What she needs is a good optometrist. But I couldn't manage to get a laugh out of her, though she did lighten up a little when I told her I'd go shopping with her again tomorrow. I have math to study, but I can't leave her alone in the state she's in!

⑤ Monday

I told Will all about Irma's latest obsession. Will says she probably needs a little reassurance and support from friends. As far as friends go, Irma's got no problem; she's got the four of us. But how to reassure her? We'll have to see. Tonight we'll get on the phone to send the SOS out to Taranee and Cornelia, too. If we put our heads together, we're bound to come up with something to help Irma. Oh, I forgot: the result of today's second round of store-hopping? Zilch!

That means our SISEP (Save Irma's Self-Esteem Plan) had better work!

⑥ *Tuesday*

YES! The SISEP worked! Here's what happened: This morning Irma met Taranee "by chance," and "by chance" Taranee told her that her brother and his friends think Irma's really cute (which was not a lie: last night it took Taranee two hours to squeeze it out of him). After that it was my turn. I showed her the picture of a dress that I had drawn last night, just for her. She was really happy, especially because I tried to follow her description of "the dress of her dreams." And she was even happier when Will told her that her mother knows a dressmaker who can make it for her! The best part was when Cornelia, taking a look at the drawing in my notebook, said, "It'll look great on Irma." At that point, however, it seemed as if Irma knew something was up. She looked all four of us straight in the eye and said, "Okay, you win! Let's go celebrate my super new look with an ice cream after school!"

THE ORACLE SAYS . . .

If you think a friend has a problem, whether big or small, the first thing to do is . . . help! Even if you don't know just what you can do to help, simply being there and listening to her will mean a lot to her.

Together you may or may not find a solution, but it's still important to listen. Maybe you can distract her, make her smile, or just let her know that you are there.

But do keep in mind that there are some problems that need adult help. If this applies to your friend, you must convince her to go to her parents about it, or to a relative or a teacher she trusts.

FIVE WAYS TO BOOST A FRIEND'S MOOD

WILL: I take her for a walk to our "special" place.

IRMA: I treat her to her favourite flavour of ice cream.

TARANEE: We look at our favourite photo album together.

CORNELIA: I lend her that sweater of mine she likes so much.

HAY LIN: We listen to our favourite song together – and sing along!

FRIENDLY TIPS:
When a Friend Feels Blue

- Call her and talk to her so she can get whatever's bothering her out in the open.

- If she doesn't want to talk about it just then, let her know you'll be there to listen whenever she's ready.

- Give her a small present.

- Send her an e-mail to let her know you care . . . and to make her laugh.

- Get her involved in something fun and exciting.

- Just remind her that you're there for her!

CHAPTER THIRTEEN

BOYS AS FRIENDS

⑤ *Sunday*
The Ice Cream Shop

Will: This is the perfect way to spend a Sunday.

Irma: And when my double-chocolate-fudge sundae gets here it'll get even better!

Cornelia: For once, I agree with you!

Hay Lin: Have you seen who's sitting over at that table?

Irma: That's Liza and Rudy. They're sitting there like two little lovebirds!

Cornelia: I didn't know they were going out.

Irma: What juicy gossip!

Hay Lin: I thought Liza had a crush on Jonathan.

Will: She still does. I heard her talking about him yesterday.

Irma: Yeah, but what about Rudy?

Taranee: They're just friends.

Cornelia: What? How can you be friends with a boy?

Irma: **Look at Martin and me. It's not like he's my boyfriend!**

Cornelia: Martin is a special case. Besides, he doesn't count. He's head over heels in love with you!

Irma: **What does that have to do with it? He's a nice guy, he knows how to listen. . . .**

Cornelia: Okay, you win. Maybe Martin isn't as immature as all the others, but . . .

Taranee: **Cornelia, boys aren't as different from us as you might think.**

Will: True. At my old school I was friends with a guy, Tom, who was on the swim team with me. We had a lot of laughs together.

Cornelia: **And there was no romance? No flirting?**

Will: No way! I liked hanging out with him because he was lots of fun. He was always pulling practical jokes. He cracked me up.

Cornelia: **That's the catch. Guys can be fun, but you can't talk to them the way you can talk to a girlfriend.**

Will: I don't agree. Maybe you can't ask boys for advice on what kind of lip gloss to buy, but you can talk to them about other stuff.

Irma: **Martin tells me stuff, and I tell him things. It's a big help, believe me. It gives you a whole other way of seeing things.**

Taranee: Boys look at situations differently. Sometimes that helps to get another perspective.

Hay Lin: **What do you mean? Are you saying that boys are insensitive?**

Will: I think boys can be sensitive and give good advice.

Taranee: **I agree.**

Irma: That's what I was trying to say. And I think it's good for us to have male friends, too.

Cornelia: **Maybe you're right, but I don't know if I could handle having a male friend.**

Will: Well, it takes a lot of patience . . . and tolerance. And you've got to be extra careful when you talk about feelings, because they'll close up like clams!

Taranee: **For sure! And most of all, never tease them in front of other boys!**

Cornelia: I guess so, but it's still hard for me to understand them!

Irma: **And you think that you're easy to understand?**

Will: Oh, girls, how about another round of ice cream! It's on me!

WHAT CAN YOU DO IF . . .

You want to be friends with a boy?

- It'll be a snap if you like each other. Just be yourself!
- If you share similar interests, like sports or watching a TV show, let him know!
- Don't tell him what he should and shouldn't do all the time . . . he's got parents, too!

Your male friend turns into a real grouch?

- Don't run away! Sometimes boys act that way when they don't know how to solve a problem.
- Give him some time and space.
- Listen to him without bombarding him with questions.

Your male friend sees you as more than just a friend?

- Ask yourself if you feel the same way.
- Tell him honestly how you feel. But be gentle. Boys are sensitive, too!

DEAR WILL
Will isn't only a leader;
she's a great advice-giver, too.

Dear Will,
There's a boy in my class who I want to become
friends with. What can I do?
– New Friend

Dear New Friend,
Be yourself! Just be as natural and sincere as
possible. You can't go wrong with that.
🐸 Will

Dear Will,
My friend Greg is really gross and throws food at
lunch. What should I do?
– Grossed Out

Dear Grossed Out,
Duck and cover – and try not to get hit! Ask him
nicely to stop, and if that doesn't work, tell the
teacher in the lunchroom.
🐸 Will

CHAPTER FOURTEEN
FRIENDS & PARENTS

FROM WILL'S DIARY:

◉ Wednesday

Wow! Summer holidays are just around the corner! I can't wait to leave for the mountains. My mum's rented a house for us for two months, together with the Nelsons, old friends of the family. Katy Nelson is my age. She's kind of a "Little Miss Perfect," but we've always had a blast together.

◉ Friday

I just got an e-mail from Katy. She's really bummed because when Mrs. Nelson said Katy could invite one of her friends to the mountains and Katy mentioned Diane, one of her classmates, her mother hit the roof! Apparently Katy's parents can't stand Diane, though I don't know why.

Sounds awful to me. Katy was hurt. . . .
I understand completely!

⊚ *Saturday*

I spoke to Katy on the phone and she filled me
in on why her parents don't like Diane. It's so
crazy! They don't approve of that girl's "weird"
look. They can't stand that Katy has a friend
who dyes her hair orange and prefers oversized
secondhand clothing to designer outfits. Katy
says that Diane is cool, a good friend with lots of
interests, and even a straight-A student! But I
guess that's not enough, because her parents are
nervous that Diane'll have a "bad influence" on
her! Sometimes parents can be a real pain!

⊚ *Saturday*

Katy's parents won't let up. Yesterday they gave
her the third degree about Diane. Katy was
mortified and refused to say anything.
Sometimes I do the same thing with my mum
when she asks me a question, though it never
seems to get me very far.

⊚ *Monday*

I've been thinking over Katy's problem.

After all, it is fairly normal for parents to be a little shaken up by the idea that their daughter has a friend whose appearance is so different. I don't think words are enough to reassure them. They need something more concrete, so that they can see for themselves that there's nothing to be afraid of.

Maybe Katy's parents just need the chance to get to know Diane. I'll try suggesting it to her!

⑥ *Wednesday*

Incredible . . . I was right! Katy invited Diane to dinner at her house, and Katy says that everyone had a good time! At first, things were kind of awkward, she told me, but the atmosphere gradually warmed up. The best part came at dessert. Diane surprised everyone with an apple pie that she had baked herself. At the end of the evening, Katy's mum didn't want Diane to leave, because she was busy trading recipes with her!

THE ORACLE SAYS . . .

If your parents have doubts about friendships you have, don't get defensive. Try to understand their reasons for disapproving. They know you're growing up and beginning to make your own decisions, but they still feel the need to protect you.

It's your right to expect their respect and trust, but don't forget, it's a two-way street.

WHAT WOULD YOU DO IF YOUR PARENTS DIDN'T LIKE ONE OF YOUR FRIENDS?

WILL: I'd have my mum get to know her better.

IRMA: I'd ask for help from someone who had already been through this!

TARANEE: I'd defend her at all costs!

CORNELIA: I'd invite her over, so my folks could see for themselves that she was really a nice person.

HAY LIN: I'd ask them why and talk to my parents about their concerns.

CHAPTER FIFTEEN
ALL AGAINST ONE

(6) *Wednesday*
After school

Taranee: Hey, Will! I thought that you had swim practise.

Will: Naw, I'm not into swimming today.

Hay Lin: Is something wrong?

Will: Kinda. There's some tension on the team.

Hay Lin: I thought you said they were a great group of girls!

Irma: And what about your friend Sharon? Have you been fighting?

Will: No, no. But she's the problem.

Cornelia: Really?

Will: I like her, but she's kind of cold sometimes. If you didn't know her, you might think she was being a snob.

Taranee: Maybe she's just shy.

Will: That's the way I was when I first moved

here. Katy and I became friends very slowly, when we'd walk home from the pool. We discovered that we actually had a lot in common.

Irma: So what's the problem?

Will: Everything's okay with Sharon and *me*, but not with the rest of the team. The others have no idea how to deal with someone like Sharon. They started teasing her. I mean, the girl hardly says anything.

Hay Lin: That's awful!

Will: She's been fighting with everyone.

Cornelia: The rest of the team is excluding her?

Will: Yup. Next week we're all supposed to go out for pizza together. The others invited me but they said it would be better if Sharon didn't come.

Hay Lin: So now you've got to choose – her or them.

Will: Unfortunately, yes. What do you all think?

Cornelia: I don't think that you should ever abandon a friend!

Irma: I agree!

Taranee: But I'm sure the rest of the team must realise they are being ridiculous.

Will: I know! And the whole idea of fighting with them is awful.

Taranee: I think you should talk to the other girls on the team individually and explain to them what Sharon's all about. If they can see that it's worth getting to know her, they'll give her a second chance.

Cornelia: **And if they refuse, you'll know that they are the ones not worth being friends with.**

Will: Good idea. I'm off to the pool. . . . I'll tell you what happened later!

Later, the girls meet in the park.

Irma: **So, Will, how did your swimming-pool diplomacy work?**

Will: Like a charm! You all were right. When it comes to certain things, groups think one way and individuals another! I talked with all of them, one at a time, convincing them to give Sharon another shot . . . or at least try.

Hay Lin: **So?**

Will: Grand finale at the pizzeria next week. Sharon'll be there, too.

Irma: **That'll be a great pizza party!**

THE ORACLE SAYS . . .

When you are part of a group, it's easy to exclude people unfairly. Be careful about being part of a group that judges people without really knowing them. If a person you care about is feeling left out, speak up!

TEST
What Kind of Friend Are You?

Begin with Question 1. Then go to the question indicated next to the answer you have chosen. After you answer your second question, you will be directed to your profile question. Think about each question carefully before answering.

1. Your friend calls you in tears. You . . .
   A. Let her talk for as long as she wants, then ask her some questions to get the whole story straight. **(QUESTION 2)**
   B. Let her get it out of her system, then tell her about your awesome day. **(QUESTION 3)**

2. Your friend has just failed a quiz. You . . .

A. Commiserate with her about how hard the quiz was, and then tell her that you'd be glad to study with her for the next one. (QUESTION 4)
B. Tell her that she should have done her homework and studied more. (QUESTION 5)

3. Your friend is in love with the blondee boy in the grade above you. You . . .
   A. Try to get to know him so you can introduce her. (QUESTION 5)
   B. Try to get to know him because you're crazy about him, too. (QUESTION 6)

4. You've only got one ticket to a concert of the band your best friend loves. You . . .
   A. Give the ticket to your friend. (PROFILE A)
   B. Go to the concert, and buy a CD for your friend. (PROFILE B)

5. Your friend loses the key chain you gave her. You . . .
   A. Are disappointed, but you don't let it show; you know she feels badly; no need to rub it in. (PROFILE B)
   B. Are disappointed and don't try to hide it. (PROFILE C)

6. You haven't done your homework. The teacher
   calls on you and your friend. You . . .
   A. Make up an excuse, envying the good
      grade your friend's about to get because she did
      the assignment. (PROFILE **C**)
   B. Grab your friend's homework and read out
      the answer. (PROFILE **D**)

PROFILES

Profile A

Best Friend in the World

No doubt about it, you're one loyal friend!
You would do anything to help a friend in need.
You are loyal, supportive, and generous . . . in
short, the ideal friend. Beware, though: even if
you sacrifice a lot for others, they may let you
down. Don't forget to think about yourself!

Profile B

Great Friend

You know who you are, which is to say, a
great friend. You're a good listener and you
understand those around you. Knowing how to
put yourself in others' shoes is no small thing
(and you're very skilled at it). You always give

your support to whoever needs it, and you're always there to listen. When you meet up with someone as sweet as you are (maybe you already have) you're sure to find a friend for life!

Profile C

Almost a Friend

You're a good friend, but you haven't decided whom you can trust and whom you should watch out for. That's why you tend to remain somewhat aloof. You'd love nothing more than to become good friends with someone, only you don't know who. Maybe it's because you haven't met the right person, though if you look closely there may be a potential friend nearby.

Profile D

Friend? Hmmm . . .

Attention: at this rate you risk winning the title of "Super Unfriendly." You may not realise it, but at times you give the impression that you're interested in others only when there's something in it for you. What's more, you seem to consider yourself above everyone else. It's time to prove that you know how to be a friend. And you'll see it's worth it!